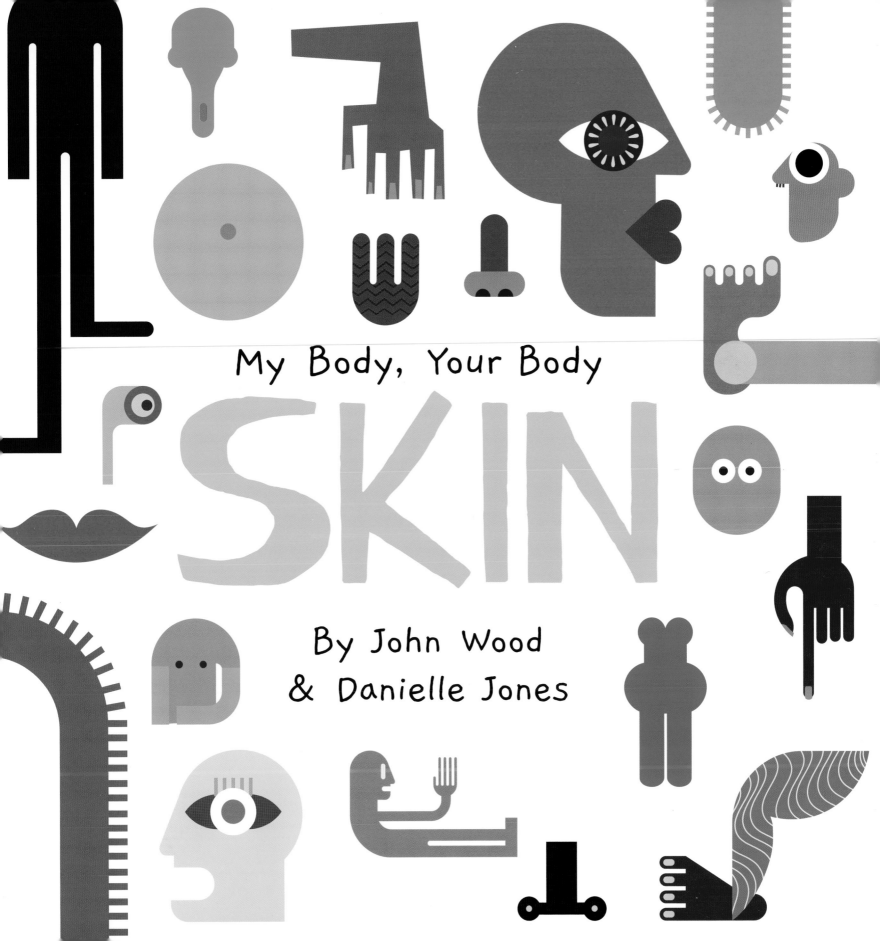

My Body, Your Body

SKIN

By John Wood
& Danielle Jones

BookLife
PUBLISHING

©2019
BookLife Publishing Ltd.
King's Lynn, Norfolk PE30 4LS

ISBN: 978-1-78637-741-8

Written by: John Wood

Edited by: Madeline Tyler

Designed by: Danielle Jones

This is my skin.

And that
is your skin.

We **ALL**
have skin.

This skin is soft,
just like

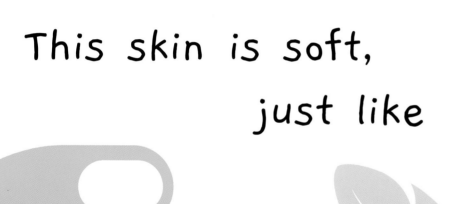

feathers
and fluff.

This skin is hard.
It is bumpy
and rough.

This skin is brown.

Oh, just look how it glows!

This skin is **dark**,
from the head

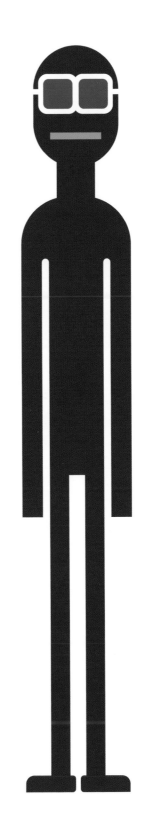

to the toes.

This skin is pink.
It is rosy and bright.

8

This skin is tanned.

And look –
this skin is white.

9

He is quite young

and his skin is

so smooth.

Her skin has wrinkles
and lines where
it moves.

This skin is covered with freckles and moles.

12

This person
gets a red rash
in the cold.

This skin is RED.
Tell us, what have you done?

Have you been sitting
outside in the sun?

15

See how this
birthmark is part
of her skin?

This boy
has got a
BIG scar on
his chin.

17

Her arms are itchy.
She scratches a lot.

His back is ticklish,
especially the top.

19

Some grown-ups'
skin has got
drawings
or words...

20

...or beautiful pictures or things they have heard.

21

Some skin
is **speckled**
with patches
of white.

22

Some cheeks are ROSY
and ruddy and bright.

We would go on.
Oh, if only we could!
All skin is **different** and **lovely**
and **good.**

24